*C*OMPILED BY THE ROYAL NATIONAL THEATRE WITH the active participation of Joan Plowright, Olivier's widow, and Richard Olivier, their son, this volume commemorates and celebrates one of Laurence Olivier's greatest achievements: the founding of Britain's National Theatre and the remarkable work he did there as director and actor.

Concentrating on these 'National Years' (1963–73), the book contains some thirty short memoirs by Olivier's closest colleagues alongside an equal number of rarely seen photos from the National archives showing Olivier on and off stage, in rehearsal and performance. Most of the contributors are themselves actors and directors, many now famous, but there are also revealing reminiscences from unsung collaborators behind the scenes.

The volume is introduced by John Mortimer and ends with Kenneth Tynan's brilliant portrait of Olivier in rehearsal for Othello. Finally, there are full production details of all the National productions that Olivier played in or directed.

The emphasis throughout is on Olivier *at work*. The result is a book which not only celebrates a great actor, director and man of the theatre but also offers candid and beguiling insights into his working methods.

The National Theatre's rehearsal room at Aquinas Street

O L I V I E R

at W O R K

The National Years

AN ILLUSTRATED MEMOIR

COMPILED BY THE ROYAL NATIONAL THEATRE

WITH *RICHARD OLIVIER*
AND *JOAN PLOWRIGHT*, THE *LADY OLIVIER*

EDITED BY LYN HAILL

ROUTLEDGE
A THEATRE ARTS BOOK
NEW YORK

Acknowledgements

Grateful thanks are due to all the contributors, and to the photographers whose work appears in these pages and who are individually credited alongside their pictures. Thanks also for their help to Rosemary Wilton, Andrew Snell, Editor of BBC TV's *Omnibus*, and to his team for use of interviews made for their *Tribute to Laurence Olivier*; to Al Senter for interviews specially conducted for this book; to Kathleen Tynan and Nick Hern Books for permission to reprint Kenneth Tynan's article on *Othello* from the collection of his *Profiles* © copyright 1989 by the Literary Estate of Kenneth Tynan; to Arthur Miller, his British publishers, Methuen, and his American publishers, Grove Press, for permission to reprint the extract from his autobiography, *Timebends*, © copyright Arthur Miller 1987; to Janet Macklam; and to Giles Croft, John Langley, Stephen Wood and Liz Curry of the Royal National Theatre.

St. James's Players Ltd

St. James's Players Ltd is a non-profit company set up by Larry during his management of the St. James's Theatre. In recent years its funds have been used to aid worthy causes in the arts world. We are very pleased that the sales of this book will benefit St. James's Players Ltd – and we hope that its work may continue.

R.O.

CONTENTS

Preface by Richard Olivier   7
Foreword by David Aukin   8
Introduction by John Mortimer   9

William Gaskill   14
Joan Plowright   16
Peter Wood   18
Anthony Hopkins   19
Diana Boddington   20
Ivan Alderman   22
Leonard Tucker   24
Maggie Smith   26
Billie Whitelaw   28
Arthur Miller   30
Geraldine McEwan   32
Edward Hardwicke   36
Michael Gambon   38
Edward Petherbridge   40
Alan Bates   42
Anna Carteret   44
Robert Stephens   46
Robert Lang   48
Jonathan Miller   50, 71
Jeremy Brett   52
Harry Henderson   54
Tom Pate   56
Michael Hallifax   58
Sheila Reid   59
Michael Blakemore   60
Denis Quilley   62
Ronald Pickup   64
Franco Zeffirelli   66
Trevor Griffiths   68
Gawn Grainger   70
Michael Caine   72
Kenneth Tynan on *Othello*   75

Afterword by Richard Eyre   83

Cast lists   86–110

Richard Olivier

Of all the kind words spoken to me about my father these last few months, the ones that have, perhaps, meant the most came from my uncle, Robert Plowright. He said to me:

> "Larry was a very special man – before I ever met him, my wife and I would go and see him perform and come away, not just impressed by his huge talent, but inspired to do our own work better. . . ."

For me, these pages are a record of the inspiration that is Larry's legacy – and of his proudest achievement – the creation of a National Theatre. If this book can continue, to whatever extent, this work of inspiration, it will have been a truly worthwhile effort. . . .

OPPOSITE

Laurence Olivier and Joan Plowright during filming of
THREE SISTERS*, 1970*

DAVID AUKIN

Executive Director of the Royal National Theatre since 1986

THE PURPOSE OF THIS BOOK IS STRICTLY LIMITED. It is to record the impact of the great man on his colleagues, people he'd meet on a daily basis: actors, designers, writers, stage managers, fellow directors, and house-keepers: the men and women with whom he made theatre. And because we cannot possibly cover all his career we have limited ourselves to those years when he was the director of the National Theatre.

We felt it was appropriate to produce this book swiftly, and should therefore like not only to thank those who have contributed to it, but to apologise to the many people who should have been included and whom it was impossible to contact in the time.

Assessments may vary about his qualities as an actor but we, in this book, can give witness to the undeniable influence he had on us all by the sheer strength of his personality, itself a product of his extraordinary talent. Above all he had, it seemed to me, the gift of being able to raise everyone he met to his level, so in his presence we were all stars. Story after story confirms this, and my own particular favourite is his first encounter with Anna Calder-Marshall, who was playing Cordelia, during the televising of *King Lear*. "Dear Sir Laurence, please do tell me anything you think I should know." "Ah," said the great man, "do you know where babies come from?" "Yes I do. I've just had one." "Oh blast," he replied, "I wanted to be the first to tell you."

JOHN MORTIMER

Translated A Flea In Her Ear *for the National at the Old Vic, 1966; adapted* The Captain of Köpenick, *1971; was a National Theatre Board Member from 1967–1989*

THE GREAT ACTORS OF OUR CENTURY ENJOY AN immortality denied their predecessors. We must take the magic of Edmund Kean on trust from Hazlitt. We must make what we can of Irving from the strange, crackling intonations of an old recording. But Gielgud, Olivier and Richardson will live indefinitely on film and tonight you can pick up a video and summon up Hamlet or Henry V, or Richard III or Othello – many of Laurence Olivier's finest performances. The actor, happily, is still with us. It's the man, the artist behind the scenes, the fellow worker that this book is designed to record. The charming, loveable, sometimes manipulative, occasionally infuriating, superhumanly energetic, periodically falsely modest, usually superbly confident genius who gave birth to the National Theatre is what this book is here to record.

All these recollections are personal. My own begin at the Old Vic but they go back to my childhood before the war. I sat beside my father and saw *Hamlet* in what used to be known, as though it were in some way an unusual experience, as its entirety. I can remember everything about that production: the shape of the set, the taste of the coffee and sandwiches during the long interval and Olivier's surprising, exciting, nervous and energetic way with the verse, which my father, as usual, recited half aloud from the front row of the stalls for his assistance. I remember the *Richard III* I saw at a matinee on a half term holiday from school and the amazing first *Coriolanus* where he died and rolled down a long flight of steps almost into our laps. I never dreamt then that I should meet him as a member of the Board of the National when it was at the Old Vic, or sit for hours with him and Albert Finney in one of the Nissen huts which housed its first offices, eating apples, drinking champagne and arguing our way through every line of my translation of Feydeau's *A Flea In Her Ear* to make sure that the laughs were in exactly the right place. I never thought that I should write a play about my dead father and have to read it aloud to Laurence, who was about to play the part. "That is by far the most terrible reading of a play I have ever heard," he was kind enough to say on that occasion.

The great quality in his acting, it has often been said, was danger. The risks he took, sometimes physical (the great leap at the end of *Hamlet*, another *Coriolanus* dying hung upside down like Mussolini), sometimes emotional (as when he became, for a minute, an old female jazz singer in *The Entertainer*), were always unexpected yet never vulgar or untrue. It was the danger that produced the excitement of his performances. You had to watch him closely, every second, because you simply had no idea what on earth he was going to do next. And these magnificent moments didn't come off the top of his head; they were the result of long thought, years of observing people and thinking about them, even of visits to the zoo and watching animals. As the blinded King Oedipus he uttered a terrible, desolate scream of pain which I shall always remember, and I remember his telling me how he came by it. "First of all," he said, "I thought of foxes. Little foxes with their paws caught in a trap." He held out his wrists helplessly. "And then I heard about how they catch ermine. It was a great help to me when I heard about that. In the Arctic they put down salt and the ermine comes to lick it. It's caught when its tongue freezes to the ice. I thought about that sudden pain when I screamed as Oedipus."

He had been a young man with extraordinary good looks; you can still see the brooding beauty of his Heathcliff. He was not only a West End star in the days when the West End produced stars, but a great film star also. He brought to acting, and put at the disposal of the National, a great deal that he had learned in Hollywood. The tragic parts in Shakespeare, especially Hamlet and Lear, are full of comedy, and he used to say he learnt his timing in those plays from Jack Benny and Bob Hope. He remembered the rather portentous tone of Charlie Chaplin, who talked in his "half American half Cockney accent" and Laurence Olivier used some of his intonations to "get a nice laugh in *Othello*".

It was a combination of all these qualities, the danger, the unexpectedness, the high octane star quality, that gave the early years of the National Theatre its especial glamour and theatrical excitement. Ken Tynan, the immaculate left wing hedonist whom Laurence took on as his "dramaturge" and greyish eminence, used to say that there were Roundheads at the Royal Shakespeare and Cavaliers at the National. Certainly the National was full of dash and bravura, with occasional misguided charges at obscure plays, and many spectacular victories. Astrov, the Captain in *The Dance of Death,* and almost his last great stage performance in *Long Day's Journey Into Night,* are high among Laurence Olivier's battle honours. It's a tribute to his extraordinary power, to the stewardship of Peter Hall, Richard Eyre and David Aukin, that the feeling of glamour and excitement travelled to the National's new concrete home and can still be felt in the foyer and on the stages. It all began with him.

But what was he like? Heroic of course. For years, at the National and afterwards, he fought his illness with indomitable courage and simply wouldn't allow it to win. He swam, he dived, he acted marvellously while he could stand, and then acted sitting down. At the end, when he could no longer learn lines, he did a superb monologue on the radio. He was indomitable.

But, aside from the genius which, perhaps like all geniuses, he could never entirely understand, and the heroism, what was he like to be with, to talk to, have lunch and work with? I hope this book will tell you that. I remember him as full of jokes. The ones he liked best were the old actor laddie jokes, like the actor playing Richard III to whom someone in the gallery shouted, "You're drunk!" "You think I'm drunk?" the villainous king wandered unsteadily down to the footlights to enquire. "Well, wait till you've seen the Duke of Buckingham!" It was stories like that which made him laugh most, and he would laugh until the tears came to his eyes and his voice rose to a high tenor note of delight. Indeed, for all his star quality, that is how I shall remember him: swapping jokes and reminiscences in the way old actors have since they met for a drink in the tiring room at the Globe Theatre. The last time I saw him he was lying on a sofa at a party in his house. He entertained everybody. His legs were weak but the laughter was undiminished.

When he came to Board meetings he often treated us with mock humility, behaving like Othello before the Senate, calling us his "very notable and approv'd good masters". Naturally he didn't mean a word of it. It was all, perhaps, part of a never ending and magnificent performance.

So I hope you enjoy this book. You will no doubt find out how a great theatrical artist works, and the effect he has on those around him. You may go a long way to discovering what Laurence Olivier was like, but you may not find out everything. Under his numerous disguises he was well hidden. "Scratch an actor," he once said, "and you'll find an actor."

O L I V I E R
at W O R K

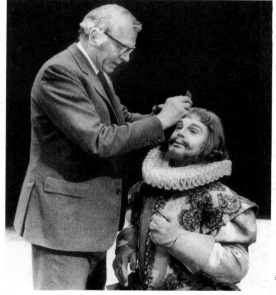

ZOË DOMINIC

Laurence Olivier adjusts the wig of Derek Jacobi at a dress rehearsal of A WOMAN KILLED WITH KINDNESS, *directed by John Dexter, 1971*

OPPOSITE

As Astrov in UNCLE VANYA

WILLIAM GASKILL

Associate Director of the National, 1963–65;
directed Olivier in The Recruiting Officer

I THINK HIS GREATNESS AS AN ACTOR AND AS A
person was that he was not at all backward looking.
All his work was for the future. At every point
in his career he seemed to identify with the
movements of theatre. Although he saw himself as
heir to Irving and Kean he created a new kind of
Shakespearean acting almost as soon as he started.

He had a pure dynamic voice that had no element
of nostalgia in it – it was only forward moving.
That's very rare. And that's why he excelled in
parts of men of action like Henry V and Coriolanus.
That sense of a man driving himself forwards was
reflected in his verse-speaking, in the way that he
carried lines through to the end, and the famous
upward inflection. . . . If you listen to it now it's a
model of accuracy – it has a steel-like quality to it.

When I directed *The Recruiting Officer* in 1963 I
was very keen on improvisation as a method of
work, having come from experimental theatre. I
told him early on that this was the method I was
going to use, and he went along with it without
any demur whatsoever. Though I don't think he
ever really liked improvising. His whole approach
to acting was to define very clearly through what
he wore – his wig, his costume and his make-up –
what he was going to be like. And if he couldn't
find what I would call the "mask" of his
performance, he wasn't at all happy. He took some
time to find the mask of Brazen, and eventually
did. I don't think he was a personality actor. I think

he was a very pure actor working on almost pure
energy and the erection of character was done
through externals.

He also had a lot of fun. He was not a portentous
or moody actor. He was lively, fresh, and funny
both on and off stage.

He made this wonderful decision to take directors
from the Royal Court – myself and John Dexter –
and inject the life of the new theatre into the
classical theatre. And this was a very bold and
strong decision. Neither of us knew him, and we
were tremendously excited and flattered to go with
the greatest actor in the foundation of the National
Theatre. In the beginning it was great fun. We
were at the Old Vic and had offices and a canteen
in a Nissen hut in Waterloo. Everything was
incredibly intimate – the walls were thin so there
were no secrets – and everything seemed very
possible. We thought the new building would be
open in about three years. In the end it took
thirteen.

With Robert Stephens in THE RECRUITING OFFICER

JOAN PLOWRIGHT

Member of the acting company at the Old Vic from 1963–74

As a very young actress, I was once asked what it was like to act with him, and I remember saying: "You don't have to act, you just react."

Not true, of course. Finally you realise that you have to act with every fibre of your being and every ounce of your skill to stay on your feet; he was constantly challenging you to be better.

He said once: "He's a good actor, very good, but he's too nice – he lacks the killer instinct."

During rehearsal for *Three Sisters* he said to me: "It's beautifully honest, sincere, absolutely truthful and straight. *Too* straight. It wants some elaboration, a bit of decoration, a bit of artifice; give them a shock every now and again to keep them on their toes. Find the one trait in the character that everyone always talks about and then go against it. They'll see it there anyhow and they'll find you much more interesting."

He liked to work on those shocks; he worked on a part like an engineer, like a sculptor and like a musician.

When we were preparing for *The Merchant of Venice*, I came upon him in the bathroom snarling at himself in the mirror; his voice sounded different and his face was red with anger and extraordinarily changed. He looked awful. He grinned when he saw me and spat out wads of cotton wool which were padded round his gums inside the upper lip. He was on the way to discovering the set of false teeth he was to wear as Shylock.

Although a great tragedian, he admired comedy more than anything in the world, and adored comediennes. He used to say that if you could play comedy you should be able to play anything. On one occasion, he said to Maggie (Smith) and me: "If you're going to get into the heavy stuff, you two girls will have to take your tongues out of your cheeks. . . .!"

With Joan Plowright in THE MASTER BUILDER *(Olivier took over the part of Solness from Michael Redgrave)*

ANGUS MCBEAN

PETER WOOD

Directed Olivier at the Old Vic in The Master Builder
and Love for Love

UNLIKE THE OTHER THREE PEOPLE RESPONSIBLE for the National's artistic policy then – John Dexter, Bill Gaskill and Ken Tynan – Larry's great secret was his upbringing in the commercial theatre. He was primarily concerned that audiences would come to the Old Vic and return. The plays he and Ralph Richardson did in their New Theatre season in the 1940s had been selected because of the parts they wanted to play, but Larry's attitude changed. He became very modest and had to be cajoled into playing Tattle in *Love for Love*. He accepted only when he was sure I wanted him.

I'm not sure if Larry had such a thing as an "aesthetic". What attracted him were bloody good plays, wonderful, theatrical situations – something to keep the audience awake at night. He belonged to an earlier age when the actor's art was to celebrate, and he looked at plays with the attitude of the vanished West End.

I think he had far fewer blindspots about certain writers or plays than most of us. I was always amazed that he was ready for anything – rather like a four-wheel drive Range Rover, custom-made to tackle any kind of terrain. When you directed him, you had to have your reasons why you wanted things done in a certain way, and he would question you, argue with you.

He had an unvarnished allegiance to his idea of the responsibility of his position. I was directing *The Master Builder*, with Michael Redgrave and Diana Wynyard, and I came into rehearsal one morning at five to ten to find Larry waiting for me. He immediately informed me that Diana had died during the night and that Celia (Johnson) would be arriving at eleven. His simplicity and directness were breathtaking. There were no wasted words. He was very good at making that kind of decision. He had been told the news in the middle of the night, and whereas most people would have waited 24 hours, Larry realised what had to be done and done quickly.

Larry had a real, almost an idealistic young man's dream about a National Theatre, peopled by the best actors in the world doing the best plays in the world. You never refused Larry – he had a natural talent for giving orders. Nobody can talk about those days at the Vic without a catch in the throat and a furtive tear, although it didn't occur to us at the time that our experience there would prove so formative. Are we being elegiac – too adulatory? Perhaps, but those were heady times.

I think Larry was the last Romantic. He wasn't a vulgarian, as some unkind people have dubbed him simply because he could please every section of the audience. And I think one of his greatest pleasures was to hear the sound of stamping feet as he came on for his curtain call. Perhaps that was his artistic policy!

ANTHONY HOPKINS

Member of the acting company at the Old Vic from 1965–72

*H*E DIRECTED ME TWICE – IN *JUNO AND THE PAYCOCK* and in *Three Sisters*. I remember his first instruction on the first day of rehearsal was that we should obey every move he gave us without question so that he could "block" the play very quickly. At the end of that first few days he'd say "Now do what you want within that structure." He'd give you enormous freedom to sort it out for yourself and find out what you wanted to do.

It sounds sentimental, but he had an amazing ability to know everyone who worked for him – he knew all the birthdays of the stage staff. He was the governor, and everyone respected and loved him. He could also be very stern because he did of course need to keep control of the great enterprise he was running. But for all his towering talent, the last thing he was was an elitist.

I got to know him quite well in later years and Jenny and I would go down to his home in Brighton, but I was always a bit dumbstruck by him and never really knew what to say to him.

Working at the new National Theatre, I met electricians and stagehands who had worked at the Old Vic and they had never forgotten those days and the sense of privilege in working for Olivier. It was the end of an age.

DIANA BODDINGTON

*Stage Manager for Olivier from the 1940s, and with the
National Theatre from 1963–88*

OUR FIRST ENCOUNTER CAME OVER THE
footlights of the Lyric Hammersmith. "My name's
Olivier," he said. "Are you Diana?" All I could see
was Heathcliff.

I then worked with him at the New, at the
St James's in 1950, then on Rattigan's *The Sleeping
Prince* at the Phoenix, and then for the opening
season at Chichester. He thought I'd be too tired
for *Hamlet*, so I didn't join him at the Vic until
Love for Love.

He was absolutely fabulous to work with. He knew
what he wanted, and he was excellent at showing
actors how to achieve it. His way of producing a
play was incredible. Before the first Chichester
season, when he was going to direct *Uncle Vanya*,
I used to go down to Brighton and he had every
move of the play blocked, using little cardboard
models in different colours. I wrote the moves
down, and when we opened that play, he had only
altered three moves.

Diana Boddington with Olivier in 1964

FIRE EXIT

PUSH BAR TO OPEN

RODDY McDOWALL

Ivan Alderman

National Theatre Head of Costume from 1963–83

H<small>E ASKED ME TO JOIN HIM AT</small> C<small>HICHESTER TO</small> set up the kind of costume production department which I had formed under Tyrone Guthrie at Stratford, Ontario. I did so, and was then asked to go with him to the Old Vic when the National moved in. I'd vowed never to work there because there was never enough money to do things properly, and I simply wasn't interested in stinting. But he was one of the few people to understand about costume production. He had made the theatre his life's work and he knew every facet. He knew how difficult costuming can be, but gave me enormous trust and carte blanche to do what I thought best. His suggestions were always so helpful and right – he was such an expert on little tricks to aid period detail, yet he would always be interested in what you had to say.

Helping him turn into Othello was very tricky. At first it took four hours for him to get ready, but we gradually got it down. He applied various layers of make-up and then polished it, but he was always afraid of it coming off on Maggie.

"When it comes to costume," he said to me one day, "you people aren't handling dead material, you're handling live humans, and you've got to cope with individuals. It's one of the most difficult sides of the business."

He was always willing to economise, suggesting ways of re-using stock. If actors complained about wearing old costumes, all you had to tell them was that Sir Laurence had worn these shoes or that hat, and their faces would light up.

Never was there a production when you didn't get a card on opening night, hand-written with a different message for everyone. It was simply a way of letting you know how much he appreciated your contribution and thanking you for what you'd done.

With a member of the wardrobe staff

LEONARD TUCKER

National Theatre Lighting Manager from 1963–85

I'D FIRST MET SIR LAURENCE WHEN I WAS JUST sixteen, working as a junior electrician on his *Richard III* production at the New (which is now the Albery) in 1944. I was responsible for the ghostly green lighting which accompanied the phantoms' visit on the eve of Bosworth. A light had burnt out, and I had replaced it with the first green I could find. Waiting in the wings, he looked at the spot, then looked at me, and I knew I'd been sussed. There was only the most subtle change of shade, but he knew the difference.

Nearly twenty years later, we met again, when he arrived to take over the Old Vic where I was chief electrician.

He was the most specific technician of any director I ever met. His homework could not be faulted. He knew how to build a crew around him in whom he had faith.

I heard him describe me as "Old Tucker who lights actors," and I lit him many times. One day, however, when I was working on a production which did not involve him, he came silently up behind me and whispered, "Bring it up, dear boy, I can't see them." Ten minutes later he returned. "Darling boy, I still can't see them." After five minutes he was back in a rage worthy of Richard III. "Bring the fucking lights up. If you could fucking see them, you might fucking hear them!"

The opening production of *Hamlet* with Peter O'Toole was a technical nightmare, and so he would come on stage in front of the curtain to apologise to the astonished audience for the production's shortcomings – often disappearing into the gravedigger's hole as he did so.

He demanded as much from you as from himself. Originally he planned to have eight different productions a week in repertoire, which meant three all-nighters, and I remember coming home at four o'clock in the morning, having to switch off the engine and coasting to my front door to avoid disturbing the neighbours.

He took notice of everyone – sending my wife Val flowers when our daughter was born. I had a love for him almost as deep as for my family. What more could one want? He basked in my spotlight and I basked in his.

In the wings at the Old Vic with director John Dexter

Maggie Smith

Member of the acting company at the Old Vic from 1963–70

LARRY WAS ALWAYS IN HIS DRESSING ROOM AT least three hours before every performance of *Othello* – his make-up was a painstaking, tedious business – applying layer upon layer of black make-up all over and finally polishing it with a chiffon scarf.

I would always call in and see him about an hour before the half, just to say hello and more often than not to help him put on his false eyelashes – and also get my notes. Desdemona was my first leading Shakespearean part and I was terrified, but he was always helpful and told me to be courageous.

One particular night I went in as usual and we talked of this and that – he was buffing away with the chiffon. Then he said: "Darling Mageen, you must, must take care with your vowels." I glued his eyelashes on and we looked at each other in the dressing room mirror. The effect was stunning. "How now Brown Cow," I said very slowly. "That," he said, "is much better." Well it was a weak joke, I thought, why should he find it funny?

It was later that evening, Act II Scene I, the arrival in Cyprus – his next line was: "Honey, you shall be well desired in Cyprus." He took my hand and swirled me about and said: "Honey, you shall be well desired in . . ." his eyes rolled and his mind had gone quite blank, but the joke had finally hit home, then he said with full force and total conviction and courage: ". . . PARIS!"

Rehearsing OTHELLO, *with Maggie Smith*

BILLIE WHITELAW

Member of the acting company at the Old Vic from 1964—66

I'D NOT DONE SHAKESPEARE BEFORE, AND TO GO on stage with that Rock of Gibraltar was very terrifying. He asked me to go to his dressing room one evening, and he had all Jocelyn Herbert's designs for Desdemona's costume laid out. He said, "There, you silly girl, that's what you're going to look like. That's 75% of it. Go home and learn the part." And that helped.

With Billie Whitelaw, who took over from Maggie Smith as Desdemona, 1965

ARTHUR MILLER

Author of The Crucible, *which was directed by Olivier
at the Old Vic, 1965*

OLIVIER WAS DIRECTING *THE CRUCIBLE* IN
London, and for two months we had been in
correspondence about a dialect for the characters.
His production, with Colin Blakely as Proctor and
Joyce Redman as Elizabeth, had a nobility that was
at once moving and austere. The actor playing the
octogenarian Giles Corey made me wonder how
such an aged man could still possess such energy,
but he turned out to be in his twenties. What I
would not forget was a long silence at the beginning
of the second act when Proctor enters his farmhouse
and washes up and sits down for dinner. It must
have lasted many minutes as Elizabeth served him
and then went about her chores, the absence of
speech itself the proof of their hurt pride, their
anger with one another, and somehow their mutual
regard, too; and at the same time it drew the
mounting fear of what was happening in Salem
Town into this house. From such exactness, what
passion!

Welcoming Arthur Miller to the Aquinas Street offices, 1965

GERALDINE McEWAN

Member of the acting company at the Old Vic from 1965–71

HE DIRECTED ME JUST ONCE, IN *AMPHITRYON 38*. I was playing Alkmena who thinks she is with her husband when he is really Jupiter in disguise. We had done our first run-through of Act One and he was pleased that I'd discovered the key to the humour. "All you've got to be now," he told me, "is like a marshmallow", which conveyed exactly the soft, malleable, flirtatious character I was playing.

When we were rehearsing *Love for Love* I referred to my son Gregory without giving the final syllable the proper stress. "You must roll all your Rs," said Larry. "Particularly when they come at the end of the word." I tried it (not with all my lines) and it did bear fruit. He was usually right about everything. He insisted that I have another dress for the last scene in *Love for Love*, and, although I never want any changes, he was right in the context of the play.

Eyes, of course, fascinated him. I'll always remember coming on for the first scene of *Love for Love* without make-up, since it wasn't considered necessary. To my astonishment, the three men – Larry, John Stride, and Bob Lang – were all flashing their made-up eyes at me. I'm not sure if Larry didn't have false eyelashes on.

There were plans afoot in 1970 to stage *Guys and Dolls*. [The planned production was later cancelled]. Larry told me I was to play Miss Adelaide. "But Larry" I said, "I'll have to learn how to sing and dance." "You'll be able to do that," he said briskly, "But make sure you get the accent right."

I was up to my eyes, and thought Larry was even more busy, so I didn't have great hopes when we got together to rehearse the *Sue Me* number. Of course, he was sensational. There was Nathan Detroit to the life, and we had a wonderful couple of hours together.

He was always encouraging us not to be too careful, to have the courage to be reckless. And he never expected anyone to be prompted on stage. He allowed for human fallibility of course, but if you got into a hole, you had to get out of it yourself.

With Geraldine McEwan in LOVE FOR LOVE

Suzanne Vasey, Olivier and David Ryall, rehearsing
A FLEA IN HER EAR

Rehearsing A FLEA IN HER EAR: *Olivier, Albert Finney,*
Kenneth Mackintosh

ZOË DOMINIC

35

EDWARD HARDWICKE

Member of the acting company at the Old Vic from 1964–71

ONCE DURING REHEARSALS FOR *OTHELLO*, I WAS sitting on a rostrum when, to my horror, he came up and sat beside me. You never quite knew what to say to him but, after we had exchanged gossip, I took my courage in both hands and told him how much I had admired his performance as Coriolanus at Stratford – particularly that awesome leap fall. He was so delighted by this compliment that his face lit up like a child's, and I suddenly realised that he still wanted and needed the occasional word of praise. He was usually so busy patting everybody else on the back that nobody thought to do the same to him.

It was impossible to predict what he would say next. He would often sit down beside you in the canteen and come up with the most obscure remarks. He once told me over a plate of salad that the finest thing to come out of the Second World War was Spam!

I owe him so much. I had taken over in *Love for Love* and was doing a comic scene, being chased by Lynn Redgrave. Larry remembered this when he put my name forward for *A Flea in Her Ear*, and so I played the character with the cleft palate and had my first big success. The production was such a tremendous hit that Larry was determined to get involved with it. He decided to take over as the butler. With bated breath, we all waited to see what he would do with it. On he came, not only with a Hitler moustache, but also with a pair of false teeth.

Since my character had a cleft palate, it was respectfully pointed out to him that perhaps his false teeth were a bit excessive. He was like a small boy deprived of his sweets, so downcast was he.

I remember meeting him in Brighton, after I had left the National. I was doing some filming before going down to Bristol to play Astrov in *Uncle Vanya*, and I had nipped into Woolworths to buy a few things. Suddenly I caught sight of a familiar figure, and greeted him. Remembering he had had such a success in the part, I asked for his advice. He reflected for some time.

"What can I tell you?" he said. "Except that he wears glasses."

As Plucheux in A FLEA IN HER EAR

MICHAEL GAMBON

Member of the acting company at the Old Vic from 1963–67

I WAS A VERY JUNIOR MEMBER OF THE COMPANY
– from *Hamlet* in 1963 to the beginning of 1967.
What I remember most about Sir Laurence is his
physical presence. He was born to be an actor. He
was the right shape – he *looked* right on stage, no
awkward corners. Also the way he dressed. He
nearly always wore suits, beautifully cut, with
broad shoulders and narrow hips. He looked
triangular. I loved his hands. He had a particular
way of holding them, bent at the knuckle. And he
wore his watch loose so that it fell onto his hand.
He also wore a copper band on the other wrist – I
suppose for rheumatism – and I noticed a lot of
other actors started to wear copper bands after that.

We were all completely in awe of him. He knew
everyone's name, and if he spoke to you, it altered
your life for days. I remember once when we were
in Birmingham with *Juno and the Paycock*, a few of
us went to the local Kardomah with Sir Laurence
for a coffee and a Danish pastry, and I thought this
is great – here I am walking along the street with
the greatest actor in the world. But the annoying
thing was no one recognised him – no reflected
glory.

JUNO AND THE PAYCOCK *rehearsal, with Caroline John*

38

Edward Petherbridge

Member of the acting company at the Old Vic from 1964–70

THE IMPACT OF BEING IN A REHEARSAL ROOM with him for the first time, when I joined to walk on in *Othello*, was a bit like being in love: the obsession one had with him – thinking about him all the time. I remember a rehearsal for *Othello* at Chichester, when Billie Whitelaw was taking over from Maggie Smith as Desdemona. I was watching because I was understudying Iago. All the scenes where he wasn't with her, he just "marked". But when he marked that performance, every single nuance, every emotion, every idea and action were all there. It was like the most brilliant pencil sketch, and then in the evening you had the oil painting. That showed the amazing technique, something which has been described as a great steel safety net, out of which a performance could never slip because it was held so firmly.

Watching rehearsals of *The Dance of Death* – again I was understudying – I would think he was giving everything. Then there was a run-through, and I realised, no, he hadn't been giving everything. I can only describe it like this – you'd been aware of the galleon, and the rigging, and the sails. Now there was this *wind*.

In THE DANCE OF DEATH

ALAN BATES

Played Vershinin in the film version of Three Sisters, *1970*

D URING THE FILMING OF *THREE SISTERS*
(which he was directing) we'd shot a scene I was in,
and Olivier said it was marvellous – go and see the
rushes with Joan (Plowright). I did, and didn't like
it, and Joan told him I wasn't happy with the scene.
He was rather displeased, and said, "Well there
isn't time to reshoot it." It was quite a chilling
moment, and I was very sorry I'd mentioned it –
questioned his judgement. Anyway, I forgot about
it, and days later – five minutes before the studio
closed – he said very loudly and sharply, "Oh, we
have five minutes, and we're going to do Alan's
re-take." So I pulled myself together and did it.
Next day he said, "What did you think?" and I
said I thought it was much better. "Oh fine," he
said.

I love the story because he had to stay in charge of
the situation – he'd had his judgement questioned,
and he'd had the generosity to give me the time to
do it again, on his own terms.

During filming of THREE SISTERS

43

ANNA CARTERET

Member of the acting company at the Old Vic from 1968–76

HE GAVE ME TWO PIECES OF ADVICE I'VE ALWAYS remembered: don't play it like a supporting actress; and if you think you've found the right inflection, don't use it. He had a great love of anything bawdy, and relished words. His approach was always audacious, and his attention to detail meticulous. On *Saturday Sunday Monday*, when he was playing the hat-maker grandfather, he went to stay with Franco Zeffirelli and visited a hat-maker to learn exactly how the work was done. I was playing the maid, and he used to pinch my bum a lot. Even into his eighties he was still the most attractive man I've ever met.

ZOË DOMINIC

Olivier's production of THE ADVERTISEMENT:
Joan Plowright, Edward Petherbridge, Anna Carteret

ROBERT STEPHENS

Member of the acting company at the Old Vic from 1963–71;
Associate Director of the National from 1968–71

I'D ONLY WORKED WITH HIM ONCE BEFORE, IN
The Recruiting Officer, when we only had one scene
together. So when I was asked to play Kurt in *The
Dance of Death*, I thought the important thing is I
will have six weeks to observe him at very close
quarters – I'll see how he does it in this huge part. It
was amazing to see how he just put it all together.
He'd try something, throw it out, try something
else. Then fine it, hone it down, slowly slowly
shape it. Put things in, then discard, discard, discard.
That was worth a million pounds to me – to watch
that process closely. Thinking: what's he going to
do today? Oh, he's changed that bit.

He always used to say: "You must understand,
actors are magpies, they steal from people. I've
stolen from people all my life. I stole from Ronald
Colman, from Alfred Lunt, from John Barrymore
– they influenced me most as an actor."

Sometimes we did both parts of *The Dance of Death*
in one day, matinee and evening. I thought it must
be exhausting for him because he was never off
stage, always barking, shouting and behaving
abominably. But he said, "No. I love it. The best
part I've ever played (apart from Archie Rice).
This is me. I'm the Captain."

In *Home and Beauty* there was the part of a lawyer
in a ten-minute scene near the end, which Arthur
Lowe played. Arthur had to leave, and Larry said,
"I'll take it over, it's a marvellous part". As usual
he had a great disguise made for himself – huge
padding, a little false nose, a wig looking rather
like Lord Goodman, a pair of pince-nez, and played
it with a heavy Jewish accent. But (like Arthur) he
could not learn it. He'd only given himself ten days
to rehearse, and found it impossible to learn. On
his first performance, when I had to exit to bring
him on, I found him in the wings at the prompt
table, desperately repeating the lines over the book.
I said, "Come on, we've got to go on!" and he
looked up and said "This is no profession for an
adult person."

Once, in the office, he said to me, "You have one
fatal flaw – You are a terrible flirt." And I said,
"Yes I am, and I learnt from a master. You! You'd
flirt with the leaves on the trees to get what you
want."

He had enormous confidence, enormous belief in
what he was doing. Also, his performances were
iron clad, so that if you stopped him at any moment
in a performance and asked, "What are you thinking
now?" he could tell you. He'd never leave anything
to chance. I once said to him after *Othello*, "You
seem to be giving 125% of yourself." He said
"Not at all – I never give more than 95%. I keep
5% just in case."

REG WILSON

With Jeanne Watts in HOME AND BEAUTY

ROBERT LANG

Member of the acting company at the Old Vic from 1963–70

H E WAS AIMING FOR A COMPANY, NOT A HOUSE style. He wanted actors who could find their own style. He was full of little gold nuggets of advice that I had never heard before. When we shared the part of Brazen in *The Recruiting Officer*, he suggested that I should watch his performance. He was getting a laugh on an entrance, when he opened the door, turned to go, and was caught. I tried it his way and got the laugh. Later he said to me sadly that now he'd lost it, for he had broken one of his own rules – that you should keep those tricks that work instinctively a secret, even from yourself.

I remember during rehearsals for *The Crucible*, Larry took Colin Blakely aside. "Colin," he said, "I am going to give you a piece of advice so useful that you will plant violets on my grave when I'm dead. Pluck your eyebrows!" "I can't possibly." Colin replied. "Maggie [his wife] wouldn't put up with it." "Well," said Larry, "You only have one life." For Larry, the eyes were the windows of the soul and the audience had to be able to see into the actor's eyes.

He often told me to keep away from that area of the stage where another actor had been particularly good. "It's too hot," he would say. "The audience has used up this spot. Try somewhere else."

He was a great one for preparation. When we were approaching the end of the Canadian tour, it was learned that quite a few contracts would not be renewed. Larry went out of his way to recount – at least three times in my hearing – how he was sacked from *Queen Christina* opposite Garbo. He emphasised that MGM had been right to do so, had he gone on with it his career would have been ruined.

He called Ken Tynan his reference book and his education. He never wanted an intellectual approach to the theatre, his was a gut reaction. The theatre was a temple to him and he chose actors who would make good company members but who were maverick spirits. He used to say that talent was plentiful but skill rare.

He was very skilled in analysing a part – picking out moments to rest and moments to use most energy. You never felt you were acting with your boss, although there was always a certain nervousness when he would announce that he was going downstage now and this was your bit.

Robert Lang, Jonathan Miller, and Olivier: rehearsal for THE MERCHANT OF VENICE – *Lang was taking over from Olivier at the New Theatre*

Jonathan Miller

Directed Olivier in The Merchant of Venice, *1970*

*H*E WAS A CHAMELEON. HE WAS ALSO A brilliant hypnotist. He could turn his back to the audience, and they would watch no one else. He had a precision, a grace, a style, a verve, and a peculiar and energetic eccentricity which simply riveted people. They were terrified by him, in a way.

His choices were often extremely unusual – a peculiar idiosyncracy of voice, of carriage, which simply fastened the attention. He belongs to a great tradition that goes back to Burbage – there's a wonderful apostolic succession from those actors who worked with Shakespeare. He's one of that great group of immortals without whom it's impossible to imagine the English theatre.

He had, before we started rehearsing *The Merchant of Venice*, had himself some dentures made for Shylock. They were, I think, based on a member of the board of the National Theatre – and a lot of his character grew out of and crystalised around the teeth. As he wore them in rehearsal (and indeed often around the corridors to bewilder and alarm people) it was quite clear that he'd invested some emblematic significance in these teeth. His character seemed to grow outwards, from the molars, as it were. I did ask him to give up the nose he'd wanted to wear, because I thought it was a cliché, but after a while I became as attached to those teeth as he was. He had, as many actors have, an attachment to physical detail. In the court scene, he became enormously fond of the brass fastenings on his briefcase – it was a matter of great pride to him that they clicked open with a menacing sound.

With Joan Plowright, dress rehearsal for THE MERCHANT OF VENICE, *Olivier wearing the nose which was later cut*

Jeremy Brett

Member of the acting company at the Old Vic from 1967–70

H*E WAS A WORKER, AND COULD SPOT SOMEONE* who wasn't working across a room. He was very tough as a leader, you had to "take it on". He would make sure that all his equipment as an actor was ready, because then he could bounce off it. We had to run very quickly to keep up. You could watch him on stage almost literally change width and height. The most important thing when you're working with greatness is to learn from it, not to challenge it. He was an animal of the theatre, which many directors are not.

He also never forgot anyone who hurt him. Which I love him for – why get hurt twice?

Publicising the season at the Cambridge Theatre. Top to bottom: Jeremy Brett, Jim Dale, Jane Lapotaire, Anthony Nicholls, Joan Plowright, Laurence Olivier

HARRY HENDERSON

Housekeeper for the National Theatre at the Old Vic, 1963–76

He was the sort of bloke that if another war started, you would willingly say: "That's it. I'll go anywhere with him." You'd be safe with him. He was a gentleman and an ordinary chap.

He used to come down and have a go at the weights in the basement. He wanted to keep himself fit.

When he was in hospital, I rang him up and asked him how he was. Soon after that, I met an actor at the stage door who said he'd been to see Sir Laurence, just after I'd phoned, and he was in tears. I was amazed to think a man like that would be so affected by someone ordinary ringing him.

Once in the huts at Aquinas Street he asked me to make him a stool so he could put his leg up – he had arthritis I think. And also a little shelf under his desk where he could put his watch, so he could look at it during meetings without anyone knowing.

Weight-training in the basement of the Old Vic

Tom Pate

Theatre Manager for the National, 1969–79

He was always very interested in the returns – particularly if he was appearing in that night's show. He would go on stage for his first scene, have a squint around the auditorium, and a few minutes later, the internal phone would go, and it would be Sir Laurence asking for the night's figures. The thing was, sometimes he would find it difficult to come out of character during the show – so in *Long Day's Journey*, say, he'd ring with his American accent, and the next night I'd have Shylock on the end of the line, asking why there were six empty seats in Row O.

In the Old Vic rehearsal room, during LONG DAY'S JOURNEY *rehearsals*

MICHAEL HALLIFAX

*Executive Company Manager for the National Theatre from
1966–74; later Company Administrator*

LARRY WAS A REAL OLD-FASHIONED ACTOR-
manager. I remember when we were touring with
The Merchant of Venice and were playing the Opera
House, Manchester, he could recall not only the
seat prices but also the week's takings when he had
last played there.

He had an extraordinary ability to retain
information, and was concerned about every
department – every area of the National.
Everything had to be discussed in minute detail,
especially the actors' salaries, the allocation of
dressing-rooms, and, of course, casting. He even
took an interest in the colour of the leaflets. He
insisted on red and green for the Christmas season,
lighter hues for summer, and it always had to be
purple during Lent. Purple, of course, was his
favourite colour.

Every aspect of the schedule was scrupulously
monitored, and he watched his own performances
very carefully. He particularly appreciated being
scheduled to play Saturday matinees when there
was a change-over to another production in the
evening. This way, he could feel he was doing his
bit in giving up a part of the weekend, but still
have Saturday night to spend with the family.

He was a prodigiously hard worker. He would
read scripts on the train from Brighton to Victoria,
then meet his secretary at the station and deal with
urgent business on the way to the theatre. He liked
to see people over his usual lunch of cheese and an
apple. The apple was a very useful prop – he would
take a bite from it, and as he chewed he could
reflect on his answer, while the other person waited
on tenterhooks. If meetings in his office had gone
far enough, he would rise from his desk, and stand
in front of his hand-painted day-to-day schedule,
thinking aloud to himself. You'd know then that
he wasn't going to discuss anything else, and we
would take our cue, gather our papers, and leave
him to his reflections.

He insisted on auditioning every actor. He was
extremely kind, with immense patience and
understanding for what they were going through.
He was very good at encouraging people,
rewarding members of the company for their work
by giving them better parts. We eventually split
the company into A and B, and he deliberately
included himself in company B to allay fears that it
was in any way inferior to A.

SHEILA REID

Member of the acting company at the Old Vic from 1964–70

*L*ARRY WAS MARVELLOUS AT PUTTING HIS FINGER on the nub of a character. I remember he said to me one day. "Think of your bottom, baby," which made perfect sense for the tight-buttocked character I was playing. He liked you to fly in and have a go at it – he applauded daring.

Throughout rehearsals for *The Crucible*, in the emotional scene where we girls all hallucinate at the trial, we never really managed to let go. But on the day of the dress rehearsal, we received a mysterious extra call. We arrived at the rehearsal room to find Larry surrounded by bottles of wine. We had a glass or two, Larry encouraged us to have a laugh and a joke, and then suggested we try the scene again. Of course, it went incredibly well, and he then told us we were to do it again and shock the boys. It was dynamite.

He was capable of such kind actions. I had to go on for Geraldine McEwan in *A Flea In Her Ear*, and was terrified. I remember waiting for my entrance, unable to remember a single line. I was still quaking at the interval, but Larry insisted that I come down from my usual eyrie and occupy the star dressing room. I was heading straight for the script when he stopped me. "Don't bother with that" he said, "Let's have a little sip of champagne instead." After that, I went on for the second half feeling a million dollars.

He was brilliant in a crisis. When we were doing *The Master Builder* once, I threw myself at his feet and grasped him around the knees, only for my wig to get caught in his watch chain. But he was able to improvise an extension to the speech while he managed to extricate himself.

When we were filming *Three Sisters*, we were very reluctant to see the rushes, but Larry insisted. Otherwise, he reasoned, how would we ever learn to see ourselves dispassionately. "Always follow the character right through to the end of the sleeve", he said, "But remember to leave the audience wanting a little bit more."

MICHAEL BLAKEMORE

Directed Olivier in Long Day's Journey Into Night;
Associate Director of the National, 1971–76

I THINK THE MOST REMARKABLE THING ABOUT
Laurence Olivier, as an actor and as a man, was the
sheer scale of his humanity. He had the ability to
reach into himself and reveal some new facet of his
personality that we had never seen before. There
were as many Larries as the parts he played. He had
great relish as an actor.

In his office at the National Theatre, he had a
picture of Henry Irving, who in the 19th century
rescued the theatre and returned it to its proper
status as one of the great arts. Larry had worked for
Lilian Baylis when Tyrone Guthrie was director of
the company at the Old Vic. Guthrie firmly
believed that theatre could be about things other
than money and success – it could be part of what
one might call The Good Fight. That tradition
informed and fed Olivier throughout his career.

With Michael Blakemore

Denis Quilley

Member of the acting company at the Old Vic from 1971–76

*I*FIRST WORKED WITH LARRY IN *LONG DAY'S JOURNEY INTO NIGHT*. The production was an enormous hit, of course, but in rehearsals he was tending to dominate. It was automatic, however generous he was. It was happening in every act, not simply in the climactic fourth, when he performed that 40-minute tirade, so Michael (Blakemore) rather warily gave him a note. He suggested to Larry that he "play in" the first three acts, since act four was awaiting him, just as if the four of us were members of a string quartet. Larry instantly grasped the point and adjusted his performance accordingly.

He was able to compartmentalise his working life and leave his managerial worries outside the rehearsal room. Rehearsal time was concentration time: the outside world did not intrude at all.

When we transferred out of the rep of the Old Vic and into continuous performance at the New, it became a gruelling slog for him. There was a one-minute break between acts, and Larry would sit on a chair in the wings and fall asleep, so exhausted was he. I'd have to tap him gently on the shoulder, remind him which stage of the play we'd reached, and he'd go on as vigorously as ever. He loved hard graft. He was like a terrier with a part, he'd worry it until he was satisfied.

He was not quite a gent in the way the other theatrical knights were – he had a vulgar streak in him. Larry was "one of us". He tended to have occasional lapses of taste in his clothes. I was especially fond of a jolly mustard-coloured suit, which I called his Brighton Bookie outfit, and he had a beige camel-hair overcoat which reached down to his ankles and made him look square-shaped. To complete the ensemble, he would sport a deerstalker. After one *Long Day's* performance, I came out of the stage door to find him, dressed in Bookie suit, overcoat and deerstalker, at the wheel of his purple taxi with its purple interior, and something like The Ride of the Valkyries blasting from the car radio. I collapsed against the wall in helpless laughter, and he leaned out of the car window, raised two fingers, shouted, "Piss off, Quilley!", and roared into the night.

Once I got over my shyness, we became very good friends, though one didn't rush to sit at his table in the canteen, in case one was thought sycophantic. I wonder if he wasn't lonely from time to time – surrounded by a barrier which it was difficult to break down. But I never felt there was any conflict between his being an acting colleague and the man who was my employer.

With Denis Quilley, rehearsal for LONG DAY'S JOURNEY
INTO NIGHT

RONALD PICKUP

Member of the acting company at the Old Vic from 1965–73

PARTICULARLY AT THAT TIME IN HIS LIFE, WITH short greying hair, heavy glasses, tweedy jackets or suits, he looked like a bank manager. But if you looked into those eyes, that was *some* bank manager. The force of the presence became immediate as soon as you looked into those wonderful deep, blazing, hypnotic eyes, full of violence and humour. He always used to say in rehearsal, "Give me more, more, more." The glorious thing about working with him was that he gave you the space to be courageous. The generous spirit of the man came out in that context. He wouldn't mind somebody doing something outrageous which failed, as long as they had a go. As a director, he never took his eyes off the nuts and bolts, because if they were rickety, then whatever flights you wanted to soar to wouldn't mean anything, because you would come adrift.

He would always pop into rehearsals of plays that he was neither directing nor appearing in. You would suddenly be aware of his glasses glinting through the window of the rehearsal room door. Then he would enter, carrying a coffee cup, very quietly and discreetly, and move to a discreet corner in a breathtaking performance of discretion. It sounds corny, but it galvanised everybody.

I remember when we were doing *Long Day's Journey Into Night* there was a piece of business which involved a very dangerous teeter on the edge of the table, in order to unscrew an overhead lightbulb so as to save electricity. Now this was a man who was no longer young, sharing with the audience the knowledge that he was in a position of danger. But it was also dead right for the character's obsessive, manic miserliness – he was *going* to turn off that lightbulb, however dangerous it was. And he would teeter on the edge of the table, turn it off, then step back in a wonderful piece of daring: "Told you so. I could do it!"

The bulb-removing scene in LONG DAY'S JOURNEY INTO NIGHT. *Ronald Pickup seated*

65

FRANCO ZEFFIRELLI

Directed Olivier in Saturday Sunday Monday

He has always been part of my life. My entire life has been permeated by this man's personality and presence. He was the flag bearer of so many things we did not have. I'd been educated and brought up in a fascist country. He was the emblematic personality of a great free democracy. Long before the Shakespeare films, I saw *Rebecca* and *Wuthering Heights*, and finally the glorious *Henry V*. I'd been an interpreter with the Scots Guards, and ENSA organised a screening in Florence of *Henry V*. That I will never forget. The whole world was opening up for us, and this was a great moment. *Henry V* was the beginning of a new era for us.

I was asked to direct *Romeo and Juliet* in 1968 at the Old Vic. Olivier came to a schools matinee. There was my idol, among all these mad, dangerous children. And he came backstage and was very flattering, and also found some very constructive criticisms to give me.

During the following years we became great friends – one of the miracles and treasures that God has given my life. The more he loved a person, the more keen he was to see their faults cured. He was a great friend, and fun, great fun. My God – a day with Larry was essential – so full of ideas and discoveries and fun and bitchiness and criticism. That ringing silver voice is a magic sound which rings in my ears forever. And the power of his silences. . . .

He was a great manipulator of all the devices, all the tools an actor can be offered. He brought them all to perfection. For each part he became a different person. For example those front teeth he used for Shylock – they made him look like a rodent.

He never lived like a penitent. He enjoyed food and drinking. But he was the most disciplined man I've ever met. His discipline is the first secret of his success – and on top of that his genius. Steel discipline, and merciless with himself and with others – no excuses, no weakness.

Rehearsal for SATURDAY SUNDAY MONDAY:
Joan Plowright, Frank Finlay, Franco Zeffirelli, Olivier

TREVOR GRIFFITHS

Author of The Party

HE DESCRIBED THE TWENTY-MINUTE SPEECH IN *The Party* as like climbing a rock face at midnight, it's raining, and you're on your own.

He was remarkably in love with the company he'd founded. He interacted with people to an extent that surprised me. I'd thought of him as somewhat aloof inside his reputation – but not a bit of it. He hung out after the show, would drink at the bar with walk ons. He had a London cab with a driver, and would drive home to his flat and chat the night away. He really wanted to understand the universe.

He was thoughtful, studious, sometimes uncommunicative. Part of the delight in working with him was the delight he got in showing you things. He was very sly, very impish, very wicked. He was such a giant inside this company.

He was a great classical-romantic actor with occasional pebble-dashes of modernism. I knew he had a street feel to him, but I didn't know it was going to be quite as deep as it was. And I was alarmed at the prospect of having this superstar at the heart of the play. In the event, I'm still somewhat equivocal about him in that role. But there were nights when he was extraordinary, when he simply soared and became symphonic, wholly arresting. He was very good at failure, and the character of Tagg is in a sense a study of failure.

He was daring – frighteningly daring. This is sometimes confused in other or lesser actors with self-indulgence. But at his best he was over the top in a military sense, not in a hammy sense. He really did believe in going out there and taking the audience on. He wasn't a cosy actor. He fought for the "language" in my play. He told me, "You've got to remember this is the first time the word cunt has ever been uttered on the stage of the National Theatre." I said, "You're not serious?" He said, "Well at least as part of the play."

The other actors in *The Party* told me I should find a way of being on stage at the last performance, because he was giving off heat like a coke brazier. I didn't, but I watched them coming off, and it was true – the side of their face that had been closest to him was red – it would seem that they'd been burnt by his energy.

In THE PARTY. Olivier's last stage performance was in this part, on 21 March 1974

GAWN GRAINGER

Member of the acting company at the Old Vic from 1972–76

THE LAST NIGHT OF *THE PARTY*, 21 MARCH 1974, I stood behind the tabs with the other members of the cast. I could hear the applause on the far side of the curtain, masked by the weight of its plush material. Slowly it rose and we were face to face with the audience again, and the clapping hands. The applause was steady, but waiting. Something was being held back. There was an expectancy, a sensing of the occasion. We bowed, the acknowledgement continued. We turned, and from upstage appeared a man who a few moments before had been a raging political animal, a fiery Glaswegian at grips with his world, his life and his imminent death: John Tagg. But now John Tagg had been left behind the set and a different animal had appeared. There was a roll to his gait, not unlike a sailor. His suit, still in character, slightly crumpled, his shoes solid and practical, highly polished. He almost ambled towards us as the house rose and the applause, his applause, that had been waiting beneath the clapping, erupted. He had a smile on his face, a shy smile, a young person's smile, male and female all in one – completely seductive. He came to the front of the stage and the cheering began. He rose with it. He loved it. He was where he belonged. He took them in from the gods to the pit. On that night he bowed to the world. He knew it was the last time. He had danced himself to a stop. He bent down and kissed the stage. Only he could do that. His mistress, his lover. There was nothing sentimental . . . simply pure love.

Jonathan Miller

Associate Director of the National, 1973–75

ONE REMARKABLE THING ABOUT OLIVIER WAS HIS carnivorous sense of expediency. He knew if anyone had a good idea, it was worth taking up. Once he had invested confidence in you, he gave you everything and never pulled rank.

He epitomised English theatre more than any other performer, and seemed to represent England rather like Winston Churchill did. He rose to his finest hour at our finest hour. He invested a great deal of himself in his patriotic duty. He felt he was leading the National Theatre as a patriot, for the country at large, and I think people reacted to that.

He was a father to the company in every sense of the word – positive and negative. In the years I worked for the National I had all those complicated, equivocal feelings that sons have for their fathers.

He would appear in the canteen at Aquinas Street, just to be with the chaps. He must have sacrificed enormous earnings by not being in films or in the West End during those years, but felt it was a public service. Working in those sheds in Aquinas Street was like being in a small airfield or naval station of which he was Commanding Officer.

No one ever addressed him as Lord Olivier. His secretary and many of his staff called him Sir Laurence. He never bridled at being called Larry. Most people referred to him as Sir. He was surprisingly anonymous in public life. Then he underwent this werewolf change when he went on stage, and something fierce, distinctive and alarming appeared.

MICHAEL CAINE

*T*HE LAST THING I EVER HEARD HIM SAY WAS
about eighteen months ago in the lobby of the
Olivier Theatre. I said, "Do you have to pay to get
in here?" He said, "Yes I bloody well do. And I'm
going to talk to someone about that."

NOBBY CLARK

*Olivier's only appearance on the stage of the Olivier
Theatre: at the royal opening of the new building,
25 October 1976*

Appointed Literary Manager of the National
Theatre shortly after Olivier's own appointment as
Artistic Director, Kenneth Tynan (1927–80) saw his job
as encouraging the theatre to perform the whole
'spectrum of world drama'. He also persuaded Olivier
to play, among other parts, Othello, and kept a
logbook of the nine-week rehearsal period. A slightly
abridged version is reprinted here.

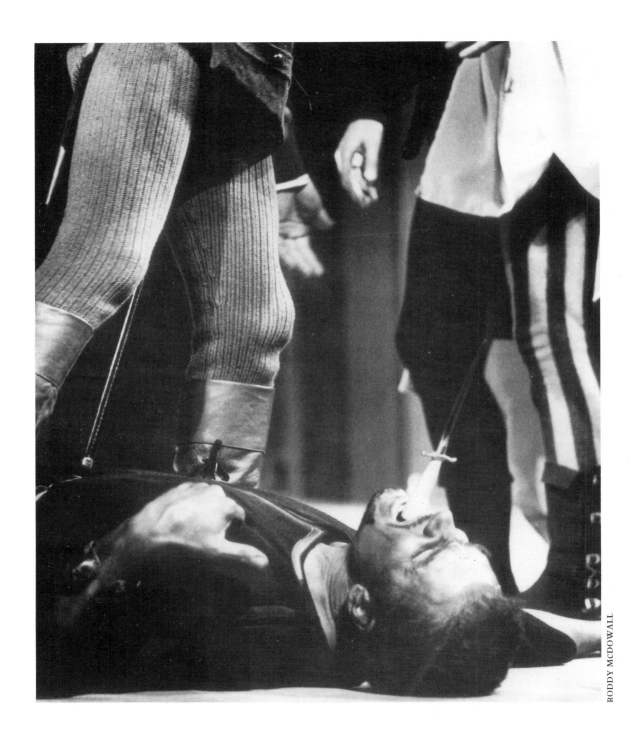

Kenneth Tynan

Literary Manager of the National Theatre from 1963–69;
Literary Consultant 1969–73

*I*T WAS NOT EASY TO PERSUADE HIM TO PLAY Othello. At least, he made it seem difficult; perhaps, deep in his personal labyrinth, where the minotaur of his talent lurks, he had already decided, and merely wanted to be coaxed. Elia Kazan once told me that the adjective he would choose to sum up Olivier was "girlish". When I looked baffled, he elaborated: "I don't mean that he's effeminate – just that he's coy, he's vain, he has tantrums, he needs to be wooed."

It took careful wooing to talk him into Othello, the only major role in Shakespearean tragedy that he had not played. He pointed out that no English actor in this century had succeeded in the part. The play, he said, belonged to Iago, who could always make the Moor look a credulous idiot – and he spoke with authority, since he had played Iago to Ralph Richardson's Othello in 1938. "If I take it on", he said, "I don't want a witty, Machiavellian Iago. I want a solid, honest-to-God NCO." The director, John Dexter, fully agreed with this approach. He and Olivier went through the play in depth and detail, at the end of which process the National Theatre had cast its Othello.

Soon afterwards I passed the news on to Orson Welles, himself a former Othello. He voiced an instant doubt. "Larry's a natural tenor," he rumbled, "and Othello's a natural baritone." When I mentioned this to Olivier, he gave me what Peter O'Toole has expressively called "that grey-eyed myopic stare that can turn you to stone". There followed weeks of daily voice lessons that throbbed through the plywood walls of the National Theatre's temporary offices near Waterloo Bridge. When the cast assembled to read the play (3 February 1964), Olivier's voice was an octave lower than any of us had ever heard it.

Dexter, dapper and downright, made a bold preliminary speech. After two or three days of "blocking" (i.e. working out the moves), there would be a first run-through with books. Of the text as a whole, he said that "this is the most headlong of the plays"; for the purposes of this production, it would be assumed that the action took place within roughly 48 hours – a night in Venice, a night in Cyprus, and a final night during which Desdemona is killed. The settings (by Jocelyn Herbert) would be sparse and simple, with no elaborate scene-changes and almost nothing in the way of furniture except the indispensable nuptial couch.

Pride, he said, was the key to all the characters, especially to that of Othello; already he was touching on the theme that was to be the concealed mainspring of the production – the idea of Othello as a man essentially narcissistic and self-dramatising.

OLIVIER'S OTHELLO

The germ of this came from a famous essay by Dr F.R. Leavis, which Dexter and I had already studied with Olivier. "Othello," Dexter told the cast, "is a pompous, word-spinning, arrogant black general. At any rate, that's how you ought to see him. The important thing is not to accept him at his own valuation. Try to look at him objectively. He isn't just a righteous man who's been wronged. He's a man too proud to think he could ever be capable of anything as base as jealousy. When he learns that he *can* be jealous, his character changes. The knowledge destroys him, and he goes berserk. Now let's have a good loud reading this afternoon."

That first read-through was a shattering experience. Normally on these occasions the actors do not exert themselves. They sit in a circle and mumble, more concerned with getting to know one another than with giving a performance. Into this polite gathering Olivier tossed a hand-grenade. He delivered the works – a fantastic, full-volume display that scorched one's ears, serving final notice on everyone present that the hero, storm-centre and focal point of the tragedy was the man named in the title. Seated, bespectacled and lounge-suited, he fell on the text like a tiger. This was not a noble, "civilised" Othello but a triumphant black despot, aflame with unadmitted self-regard. So far from letting Iago manipulate him, he seemed to manipulate Iago, treating him as a kind of court jester.

Such contumely cried out for deflation. There are moral flaws in every other Shakespearean hero, but Othello is traditionally held to be exempt. Olivier's reading made us realise that tradition might be wrong; that Othello was flawed indeed with the sin of pride. At the power of his voice, the windows shook and my scalp tingled. A natural force had entered the room, stark and harsh, with vowel-sounds as subtly alien as Kwame Nkrumah's; and the cast listened pole-axed. I wondered at the risks he was taking. Mightn't the knockdown arrogance of this interpretation verge too closely for comfort on comedy? Wasn't he doing to Othello precisely what he deplored in the Peter Brook-Paul Scofield *King Lear* (or "Mr Lear", as he called it) – i.e. cutting the hero down to size and slicing away his majesty? Then he came to "Farewell the plumed troop," and again the hair rose on my neck. It was like the dying moan of a fighting bull.

Like the cast, I was awed. We were learning what it meant to be faced with a great classical actor in full spate – one whose vocal range was so immense that by a single new inflexion he could point the way to a whole new interpretation. Every speech, for Olivier, is like a mass of marble at which the sculptor chips away until its essential form and meaning are revealed. No matter how ignoble the character he plays, the result is always noble as a work of art. I realised how vital, for an actor, is the use to which he puts the time available to him before his bodily resources begin to flag. In the last 15 years Olivier has played more than 20 stage parts, ancient and modern. During the same period Marlon Brando – once, potentially, an American Olivier – has not appeared on stage at all. He had the quality; but quantity is the practice that makes quality perfect.

Othello was rehearsed for nine weeks before it opened on tour at the Alexandra Theatre, Birmingham. For three of the nine weeks Olivier was absent, suffering from a virus infection which (as he put it) "shook me like a dog shakes a rat". Rather than follow his performance as it evolved day by day, I propose to deal with it scene by scene, using the notes I kept during rehearsals of what was intended and what was achieved.

Act I Scene ii. His first entrance: an easy, rolling gait, enormous sly eyes, and a tender-tigerish smile. It is clear from the start that whatever else this performance may be, it is going to be a closely studied piece of physical impersonation. (Odd how rare this element is in contemporary theatre: modern actors in general – as Max Beerbohm said of Duse – "never stoop to impersonation", wrongly holding it to be a facile and suspect skill.) In the opening exchanges with Iago, Olivier displays the public mask of Othello: a Negro sophisticated enough to conform to the white myth about Negroes, pretending to be simple and not above rolling his eyes, but in fact concealing (like

any other aristocrat) a highly developed sense of racial superiority. This will not be a sentimental reading of the part, nor one that white liberals will necessarily applaud.

Note on props: during the early part of the scene he sniffs at and toys with a long-stemmed pink rose. Is this a foreshadowing of the lines in v.ii.

> "... *When I have pluckt the rose,*
> *I cannot give it vital growth again,*
> *It needs must wither ...?"*

"Keep up your bright swords, for the dew will rust them" is delivered almost affably, with a trace of sarcastic condescension in the second half of the line. Othello's mere presence is enough to silence a brawl. This is a man who does not need to raise his voice to be obeyed.

Act I Scene iii. The Senate: a midnight meeting, convened in panic at the impending Turkish threat. Othello, a fully "assimilated" Moor, wears a crucifix round his neck and crosses himself when Brabantio accuses him of having won Desdemona's love with witchcraft. For the great account of the wooing, he is still and central. "Her father – loved me" is directed straight at Brabantio, in tones of wondering rebuke. There is lofty pride in the re-telling of his magical adventures; and when he reaches the line about "the Cannibals, that each other eat, The Anthropophagi," he utters the Greek word by way of kindly parenthetical explanation, as if to say, "That, in case you didn't know, is the scholarly term for these creatures." He also manages to convey his sardonic awareness that this is just the kind of story that Europeans would expect Africans to tell. (All this in a single phrase? Yes, such is the power of inflexion when practised by a master.) "She wisht she had not heard it: yet she wisht/ That heaven had made her such a man" modulates from gentle, amused reminiscence to proud, erotic self-congratulation. "Upon this hint I spake" is preceded by a smiling shrug, the actor dwelling on "hint" as a jocular understatement, and forcing the senators to share his pleasure. On "This only is the witchcraft I have used," Olivier isolates the word "witchcraft" so that you can almost hear the inverted commas, deliberately making the second vowel harsh and African, and pointedly eyeing Brabantio as he delivers it. Throughout the speech, he is at once the Duke's servant and the white man's master. Every time we rehearse it, the room is pin-still. For some of us, this is the high point of the performance.

Act II Scene i. The arrival at Cyprus, after a hot, wild hurricane that signals our entry into a world quite different from that of super-civilised Venice. Embracing Desdemona, Othello is beside himself with deep, internal joy, wreathed in smiles and barely able to speak. He greets the Cypriots as old friends; they are closer to him in blood than the Venetians.

Act II Scene iii. Contrary to custom, Iago's first song ("And let me the canakin clink") is a homesick soldier's lament instead of the usual rousing chorus: a perceptive idea of John Dexter's. The Cassio-Montano squabble develops (as Stanislavsky suggested in his notes on the play) into a popular riot, with the mutinous Cypriots rising against their Venetian overlords; thus Othello has something more to quell than a private quarrel. He enters nursing a scimitar; Iago lines the Venetian soldiers up before him as if on parade.

Act III Scene iii. The great jealousy scene, the fulcrum that thrusts the energy of the play towards tragedy. To Desdemona's pleas for the reinstatement of Cassio, Othello reacts with paternal chuckles, a man besotted by the toy white trophy he has conquered. For the duologue with Iago, Dexter deliberately makes things technically hard for both actors. Othello usually sits at a desk, riffling through military documents while Iago begins his needling; Dexter forbids the desk, thereby compelling the actors to make the scene work without recourse to props.

He is swiftly proved right. With no official tasks to perform, Othello ceases to be a sitting target, and Iago must struggle to hold his attention: both actors must find reasons deeper than accidents of duty to keep them together long enough for the deadly duologue to be irrevocably launched. Stroke of genius by Olivier: no sooner has Iago mentioned

Cassio than *he* takes the initiative. Iago seems to be hiding something, so Othello determines to quiz *him,* in order to get a full report on Cassio's character; after all, Desdemona wants the lieutenant reinstated, and the general owes it to his wife to find out all the facts. "What does thou *think?*" he asks with avuncular persistence, like a headmaster ordering one prefect to tell tales on another. On "By heaven, he echoes me," he is mock-severe, rebuking Iago for talking in riddles. His whole attitude is one of supreme self-confidence. (Query: will the public and critics realise that this is an egocentric Othello, not an egocentric performance?)

The entry of Desdemona: when Othello complains of "a pain upon my forehead," he presses two fingers above his eyebrows, indicating to us (though not to her) the cuckold's horns. At "Come, I'll go in with you," he leads her off in a close, enfolding embrace that will end in bed. During his absence, we have Iago's seizure of the handkerchief dropped by Desdemona. Note: in Frank Finlay's interpretation, endorsed by Dexter, Iago has been impotent for years – hence his loathing of Othello's sexuality and his alienation from Emilia.

When Othello returns ("Ha! ha! false to *me?*"), he has been unable to make love to Desdemona; he sniffs his fingers as if they were tainted by contact with her body. He ranges back and forth across the stage for "Farewell the tranquil mind!" The speech becomes an animal moan of desolation, the long vowels throbbing and extended, and the "ear-piercing fife" rising to an ecstasy of agonised onomatopoeia.

On "Villain, be sure thou prove my love a whore," Olivier locks Finlay by the throat and hurls him to the ground, threatening him with a trick knife-blade concealed in a bracelet. (He will later use the same weapon to cut his own jugular vein.) This assault leaves Iago hoarse and breathless. From now on Othello is a boundlessly destructive force, needing only to be steered to its target.

Act III Scene iv. The handkerchief scene. As Othello tells the story of this talismanic heirloom ("there's magic in the web of it"), we get a glimpse of the narrative spell-binder who conquered Desdemona with his tales. She sits at his feet to listen, drawn back once again into the exotic world of the Anthropophagi. These will be their last peaceful moments together. Her rueful comment on the missing handkerchief ("Then would to God that I had never seen't!") produces a sudden, terrific spasm of fury: *"Ha! wherefore?"* – the words detonate like thunder-claps. Before his exit, Othello repeats "The handkerchief!" three times. Olivier reaches a climax of point-blank intimidation in the first two, but for the third and last he finds a moving new inflexion, uttering the line like a desperate suppliant, whimpering for reassurance, his hands clasped before him in prayer.

Act IV Scene i. Othello is now Iago's creature. The new lieutenant is merely a passenger aboard the great plunging ship of Othello's wrath. "All you have to do," says Olivier to Finlay, "is toss him a bit of meat from time to time, and he gobbles it whole." Dexter to Finlay: "At this point you're like Lady Macbeth after Macbeth's killed Duncan – there's really nothing left to do except go mad." Iago and the Moor enter together and drift slowly downstage; the sinister responses and repetitions are murmurously chanted, like a satanic litany spoken in a trance:

> *"Or to be naked with her friend in bed*
> *An hour or more, not meaning any harm?*
> *Naked in bed, Iago, and not mean harm . . ."*

The two men even begin to sway gently from side to side, locked together in the rhythm of Othello's pain. In the epileptic fit Olivier pulls out all the stops; but, as always, there is science in his bravura. The symptoms of epilepsy (the long, shuddering breaths; the head flung back; the jaw thrust out) are painstakingly reproduced; and when he falls thrashing to the ground like a landed barracuda, Iago shoves the haft of a dagger between his teeth to keep him from biting off his tongue.

Othello's re-entry after eavesdropping on the Cassio-Iago scene and Bianca's intervention with the handkerchief: he circles the stage, a caged jungle king *in extremis,* with Iago immobile at the centre.

Dexter to Finlay: "Think of yourself as a ringmaster. Just give him an occasional flick of the whip – like 'Nay, that's not your way' – to keep him in order." The arrival of Lodovico from Venice: as Dexter points out, this changes the whole situation. Iago's moment of triumph is over.

Act IV Scene ii. The interrogation of Emilia (Joyce Redman) and the confrontation with Desdemona, whom Othello now openly treats as a prostitute. The scene is a nightmare of cruelty, and Olivier plays it to the hilt: the superman runs amok, the bull wrecks the china-shop. On lines like:

> *". . . turn thy complexion there,*
> *Patience, thou young and rose-lipt cherubin, –*
> *I there look grim as hell . . ."*

Olivier resorts to shrill and wailing headnotes that savour slightly of self-indulgence. Answer: it is Othello, not Olivier, who is indulging himself emotionally. Question: yes, but will the audience know the difference?

At "O thou weed/ Who art so lovely fair, and smell'st so sweet," he crawls across the stage and lies on top of Desdemona: for a moment, desire almost overcomes disgust: or rather, both emotions co-exist. Othello comes close to committing the crime of which Brabantio accused his daughter: he very nearly "falls in love with what he fears to look on."

Act V Scene ii. The killing of Desdemona in the bedroom. Entrance of Othello: white-robed and dark-limbed, picked out by a shaft of moonlight through a grille over the chamber door. On "Who's there?", Desdemona wakes up in a convulsion of fear, as if from a nightmare; then says with a sigh of relief, "Othello!" The "murder, which I thought a sacrifice" is accomplished with relentless, implacable precision; honour having been offended, the prescribed penalty must be enforced.

Turning-point of the case against Iago: Emilia can prove that her husband is a dirty-minded gossipmonger, but not until Othello reveals that he has seen Cassio with the handkerchief ("I saw it in his hand") can she prove that Iago is guilty of conspiracy to murder. It takes her a second or two to react to the implication of what Othello has said; but then she bursts out with "O God! O heavenly God!" – and after this clinching double-take it is all up with Iago, since she now reveals that she gave him the handkerchief. The end of Iago: he offers himself masochistically to Othello's sword. "I bleed, sir; but not kill'd" is spoken with quiet satisfaction. The end of Othello: kneeling on the bed, hugging the limp corpse of Desdemona, he slashes his throat with the hidden stiletto we saw in III.iii. And slumps like a falling tower.

About six months after the production opened, the Italian director Franco Zeffirelli saw it for the first time. Of Olivier's performance he said: "I was told that this was the last flourish of the romantic tradition of acting. It's nothing of the sort. It's an anthology of everything that has been discovered about acting in the last three centuries. It's grand and majestic, but it's also modern and realistic. I would call it a lesson for us all."

Joan Plowright, Laurence Olivier, Peter Hall,
Richard Eyre, outside the stage door of the National Theatre
on the evening of the NT's 80th birthday tribute to Lord
Olivier, 1987

RICHARD EYRE

Director of the Royal National Theatre from 1988,
succeeding Sir Peter Hall who was Director from 1973

*I*T IS SOMETHING MORE THAN A PIOUS SENTIMENT to say that we shall never see his like again. Like Churchill, he was a man who exactly matched the moment of history. For a catalogue of reasons to do with the spirit of the times, the all-pervasiveness of money and the market-place, the structure of the theatre, the shrinking of the film industry, and the atrophy of artistic ambition, it is inconceivable that we will see a great buccaneering actor-manager, also a Hollywood film star, shape and change the theatre so often and so judiciously as Olivier did.

When he ran the National at the Old Vic it was the best company of actors in the world, aided not a little by being in one of the very best theatres. He was bitterly disappointed not to preside over the move to the South Bank, which he described, wittily I think, as an "experiment". That experiment is his legacy – a hugely ambitious project, you might say grandiose – but a noble one.

The last time he came to the National was an appropriately epic theatrical occasion, a Gala evening to celebrate his 80th birthday. I'd only just been made director-designate of the National Theatre, and was standing rather diffidently at the Stage Door, in the ample shadow of Peter Hall, waiting for Olivier to arrive. Outside there was a dauntingly large crowd and hordes of buzzing papparazzi. The atmosphere lay somewhere between anticipation of a religious event and the arrival of Joan Collins at a BAFTA awards ceremony. As the car pulled up there was an almost Iranian wail from the crowd. Then the very large black limousine disgorged a small and very frail man, supported by Joan Plowright. There was a fusillade of flash bulbs, screams and hoots. He moved slightly towards the crowd and hesitated, wavering between what looked like absolute terror and intense joy. Simultaneously, Peter Hall was going towards him, arms outstretched, and there was a moment of confusion when Larry looked as if he wasn't quite sure who it was approaching him armed with such a benign smile. Then, recognising Peter, he shook his hand and approached me with an expression of complete and justified bewilderment, as if I was the wrong suspect in an identity parade. The three of us shuffled awkwardly into a group for a "photo opportunity". We all stared at the cameras in baffled embarrassment.

The evening proceeded like many of those charitable events. For me, the high point was at the end, when the whole audience rose and Larry stood for the applause at the side of the Olivier Theatre. Joan made several attempts to lead him out of the auditorium, but he was not to be led. He was a man for whom applause was clearly the stuff of life. He raised his right hand in acknowledgement, making a beautiful gesture like cupping butterflies, and the clapping went on and on. The audience would happily have stayed for an hour, and he would happily have stayed with them.

During Laurence Olivier's directorship of the National Theatre, he appeared in twelve plays (taking over roles in three), and directed nine. The following are the cast lists of all these, at the time of the opening (or, in the case of take-overs, when he appeared in them):

HAMLET

by William Shakespeare

Francisco	**Dan Meaden**	Rosencrantz	**Peter Cellier**
Bernardo	**Richard Hampton**	Guildenstern	**Raymond Clarke**
Marcellus	**Michael Turner**	First Player	**Robert Lang**
Horatio	**Robert Stephens**	Player King	**Harry Lomax**
Ghost of Hamlet's father	**Anthony Nicholls**	Player Queen	**John Rogers**
Claudius	**Michael Redgrave**	Other Players	**Richard Hampton**
Gertrude	**Diana Wynyard**		**Clive Rust**
First Gentlewoman	**Wynne Clark**		**Derek Ware**
Ophelia	**Rosemary Harris**		**Christopher Chittell**
Polonius	**Max Adrian**		**Alan Ridgway**
Osric	**Terence Knapp**	Fortinbras	**John Stride**
Claudio	**Martin Boddey**	Norwegian Captain	**Colin Blakely**
Voltimand	**Trevor Martin**	Sailors	**James Mellor**
Cornelius	**Reginald Green**		**Reginald Green**
Laertes	**Derek Jacobi**	First Gravedigger	**Frank Finlay**
Hamlet	**Peter O'Toole**	Second Gravedigger	**Michael Rothwell**
Reynaldo	**Keith Marsh**	Priest	**Roger Heathcott**

Court Ladies, Courtiers, Soldiers, Servants:
Sunny Amey, Rod Beacham, Elizabeth Burger, Byron Chandler, Lewis Fiander, Michael Gambon, Jeanne Hepple, William Hobbs, Jeanette Landis, Enid Lorimer, James Mellor, Bruce Purchase, Louise Purnell, Lynn Redgrave, Jean Rogers, Michael Rothwell, Adam Rowntree, Robert Russell, Clive Rust, Ann Rye, Michael Turner, Mervyn Willis

Production by	**Laurence Olivier**
Designed by	**Sean Kenny**
Costumes by	**Desmond Heeley**
Music by	**John Addison**
Lighting by	**Richard Pilbrow**
Swordplay by	**William Hobbs**

Opening: 22 October 1963

Uncle Vanya

by Anton Chekhov, translation by Constance Garnett

Marina Timofeyevna	**Wynne Clark**
Mihail Lvovitch Astrov	**Laurence Olivier**
Ivan Petrovitch Voynitsky (Vanya)	**Michael Redgrave**
Alexander Vladimirovitch Serebryakov	**Max Adrian**
Ilya Ilyitch Telyegin	**Keith Marsh**
Sofya Alexandrovna (Sonya)	**Joan Plowright**
Ilyena Andreyevna	**Rosemary Harris**
Marya Vassilyevna Voynitsky	**Enid Lorimer**
Yefim	**Robert Lang**
Production by	**Laurence Olivier**
Designed by	**Sean Kenny**
Costumes by	**Beatrice Dawson**
Guitar music arranged by	**Alexis Chesniakov**
Lighting by	**John B Read**

*Opening: 19 November 1963, having previously been seen in the first
two seasons at Chichester Festival Theatre, 1962 and 1963*

THE RECRUITING OFFICER

by George Farquhar

Mr Balance	**Max Adrian**	Drummer	**Alan Ridgway**
Mr Scale	**Peter Cellier**	Boy with whistle	**Christopher Chittell**
Mr Scruple	**Michael Turner**	Balance's steward	**Rod Beacham**
Mr Worthy	**Derek Jacobi**	Melinda's servant	**Michael Gambon**
Captain Plume	**Robert Stephens**	Melinda	**Mary Miller**
Captain Brazen	**Laurence Olivier**	Silvia	**Maggie Smith**
Kite	**Colin Blakely**	Lucy	**Jeanne Hepple**
Bullock	**James Mellor**	Rose	**Lynn Redgrave**
Costar Pearmain	**John Stride**	Poacher's wife	**Jeanette Landis**
Thomas Appletree	**Keith Marsh**	Collier's wife	**Elizabeth Burger**
Bridewell	**Michael Rothwell**		
Pluck	**Trevor Martin**	Production by	**William Gaskill**
Thomas	**Dan Meaden**	Scenery & costumes by	**Rene Allio**
A Poacher	**Clive Rust**	Music arranged by	**Richard Hampton**
A Collier	**Richard Hampton**	Lighting by	**Richard Pilbrow**

Opening: 10 December 1963

THE MASTER BUILDER

by Henrik Ibsen, adapted by Emlyn Williams

Ragnar Brovik	**Edward Hardwicke**
Kaja Fosli	**Jeanne Hepple**
Knut Brovik	**Edward Caddick**
Halvard Solness	**Laurence Olivier**
Aline	**Celia Johnson**
Doctor Herdal	**Peter Cellier**
Hilde Wangel	**Maggie Smith/Joan Plowright**
Foreman	**Ron Pember**
Friends	**Janie Booth**
	Elizabeth Burger
	Terence Knapp
	Sheila Reid
	Maggie Riley
	Christopher Timothy
Production by	**Peter Wood**
Scenery & costumes by	**Rudolf Heinrich**
Lighting by	**Brian Freeland**

Opening: 9 June 1964, with LO: 17 November 1964

OTHELLO

by William Shakespeare

Roderigo	**Michael Rothwell**	Senator	**Keith Marsh**
Iago	**Frank Finlay**	Sailor	**Tom Kempinski**
Brabantio	**Martin Boddey**	Messenger	**Peter John**
Othello	**Laurence Olivier**	Desdemona	**Maggie Smith**
Cassio	**Derek Jacobi**	Montano	**Edward Hardwicke**
Senate officers	**Edward Petherbridge**	Cypriot Officers	**William Hobbs**
	George Innes		**Roger Heathcott**
Gratiano	**Edward Caddick**		**Keith Marsh**
Lodovico	**Kenneth Mackintosh**	Emilia	**Joyce Redman**
Duke of Venice	**Harry Lomax**	Herald	**Neil Fitzpatrick**
Duke's Officer	**Terence Knapp**	Bianca	**Mary Miller**

Senators, soldiers, Cypriots: **Raymond Clarke, Neil Fitzpatrick, Reginald Green, Roger Heathcott, William Hobbs, George Innes, Caroline John, Peter John, Tom Kempinski, Terence Knapp, Keith Marsh, Ron Pember, Edward Petherbridge, Sheila Reid, John Rogers, Robert Russell, Frank Wylie**

Production by	**John Dexter**
Scenery & costumes by	**Jocelyn Herbert**
Lighting by	**Leonard Tucker**
Music arranged by	**Richard Hampton**
Fights arranged by	**William Hobbs**

Opening: 21 April 1964

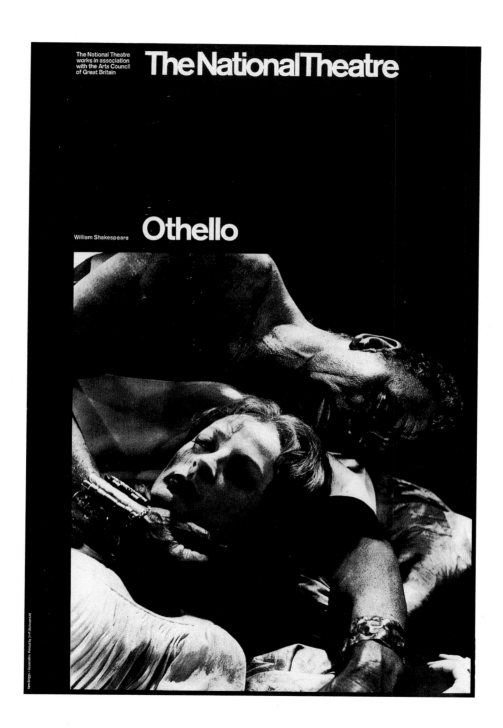

THE CRUCIBLE

by Arthur Miller

Betty Parris	**Janina Faye**	Goodwife Elizabeth Proctor	**Joyce Redman**
Reverend Samuel Parris	**Kenneth Mackintosh**	Francis Nurse	**Keith Marsh**
Tituba	**Pearl Prescod**	Ezekiel Cheever	**Michael Turner**
Abigail Williams	**Louise Purnell**	Marshall Herrick	**Michael Gambon**
Susanna Walcott	**Janie Booth**	Deputies	**Terence Knapp**
Goodwife Ann Putnam	**Barbara Hicks**		**Robert Russell**
Thomas Putnam	**Trevor Martin**		**Peter Cellier**
Mercy Lewis	**Sheila Reid**	Judge Hathorne	
Mary Warren	**Jeanne Hepple**	Deputy-Governor Danforth	**Anthony Nicholls**
John Proctor	**Colin Blakely**		
Goodwife Rebecca Nurse	**Wynne Clark**	Production by	**Laurence Olivier**
Giles Corey	**Frank Finlay**	Scenery & costumes by	**Michael Annals**
Reverend John Hale	**Robert Lang**	Lighting by	**Brian Freeland**

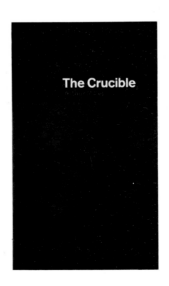

Opening: 19 January 1965

LOVE FOR LOVE

by William Congreve

Sir Sampson Legend	**Anthony Nicholls**	Servant to Foresight	**David Hargreaves**
Valentine	**John Stride**	Blackamoor	**Roy Holder**
Scandal	**Robert Lang**	Robin	**Edward Hardwicke**
Tattle	**Laurence Olivier**	Singer	**Leonard Whiting**
Ben	**Albert Finney**	Angelica	**Geraldine McEwan**
Foresight	**Miles Malleson**	Mrs Foresight	**Madge Ryan**
Jeremy	**Tom Kempinski**	Mrs Frail	**Joyce Redman**
Trapland	**Harry Lomax**	Miss Prue	**Lynn Redgrave**
Snap	**Michael Gambon**	Nurse	**Barbara Hicks**
Buckram	**Keith Marsh**	Jenny	**Janina Faye**
Steward to Sir Sampson	**Reginald Green**		

Sailors, women, servants, etc: **Petronella Barker, Anne Godley, Michael Gambon, Edward Hardwicke, William Hobbs, Roy Holder, Anthony Hopkins, Lewis Jones, Sheila Reid, Malcolm Reynolds, Maggie Riley, Malcolm Terris, Christopher Timothy, Leonard Whiting**

Production by	**Peter Wood**
Designed by	**Lila de Nobili**
Music by	**Marc Wilkinson**
Dances by	**Alfred Rodrigues**
Lighting by	**Richard Pilbrow**

Opening: 20 October 1965

A FLEA IN HER EAR

by Georges Feydeau, translated by John Mortimer

Camille Chandebise	**Edward Hardwicke**
Antoinette Plucheux	**Jane Lapotaire**
Etienne Plucheux	**Laurence Olivier**
Dr Finache	**Peter Cellier**
Lucienne Homenides de Histangua	**Maggie Riley**
Raymonde Chandebise	**Geraldine McEwan**
Victor Emmanuel Chandebise	**Robert Lang**
Romain Tournel	**John Stride**
Carlos Homenides de Histangua	**Edward Petherbridge**
Eugenie	**Petronella Barker**
Augustin Ferraillon	**Graham Crowden**
Olympe	**Margo Cunningham**
Baptistin	**Reginald Green**
Herr Schwarz	**David Ryall**
Poche	**Robert Lang**
Guests at the Hotel Coq d'Or	**Gillian Barge**
	Lewis Jones
	Peter Penry-Jones
	Frederick Pyne
	Suzanne Vasey
Production by	**Jacques Charon**
Designed by	**Andre Levasseur**
Lighting by	**John B Read**

Opening: 8 February 1966; with LO: 6 September 1967

JUNO AND THE PAYCOCK

by Sean O'Casey

Mary Boyle	**Caroline John**
Johnny Boyle	**Ronald Pickup**
Juno Boyle	**Joyce Redman**
Jerry Devine	**Michael Gambon**
'Captain' Jack Boyle	**Colin Blakely**
'Joxer' Daly	**Frank Finlay**
A Sewing Machine Man	**Reginald Green**
A Coal Block Vendor	**Keith Marsh**
Charles Bentham	**Peter Cellier**
Mrs Maisie Madigan	**Madge Ryan**
Mrs Tancred	**Maggie Riley**
Neighbours	**Petronella Barker**
	Margo Cunningham
	David Hargreaves
'Needle' Nugent	**Harry Lomax**
An Irregular Mobiliser	**Anthony Hopkins**
Furniture Removal Men	**Reginald Green**
	Christopher Timothy
Irregulars	**Lewis Jones**
	Malcolm Terris
Production by	**Laurence Olivier**
Designed by	**Carmen Dillon**
Lighting by	**Richard Pilbrow & John B Read**
Special associate	**Harry Hutchinson**

Opening: 26 April 1966

The National Theatre works in association with the Arts Council of Great Britain

The National Theatre

August Strindberg

The Dance of Death

THE DANCE OF DEATH

by August Strindberg, translated by C D Locock

Edgar	**Laurence Olivier**
Alice	**Geraldine McEwan**
Jenny	**Carolyn Jones**
Kristin	**Kate Lansbury**
Kurt	**Robert Stephens**
Old Woman	**Jeanne Watts**
Judith	**Janina Faye**
Allan	**Malcolm Reynolds**
The Lieutenant	**Peter Penry-Jones**
Corporal	**Lewis Jones**
Sentries	**Anthony Hopkins**
	William Hoyland
	Frederick Pyne
	Richard Warwick

Production by	**Glen Byam Shaw**
Scenery & costumes by	**Motley**
Lighting by	**John B Read**
Music composed & arranged by	**Anthony Bowles**
Dance arranged by	**Romayne Grigorova**

Opening: 21 February 1967

THREE SISTERS

by Anton Chekhov, translated by Moura Budberg

Andrei	**Anthony Hopkins**	Vershinin	**Robert Stephens**
Olga	**Jeanne Watts**	Fedotik	**Ronald Pickup**
Masha	**Joan Plowright**	Rode	**David Belcher**
Irina	**Louise Purnell**	Orderly	**Lennard Pearce**
Natasha	**Sheila Reid**	Officers	**Luke Hardy**
Fyoder Ilyich Kullighin	**Kenneth Mackintosh**		**Richard Kay**
Anfissa	**Wynne Clark**	Soldiers	**Alan Adams**
Ferapont	**Harry Lomax**		**Stuart Campbell**
Serving-maid	**Carolyn Jones**		**John Flint**
Maid	**Mary Griffiths**		**Luke Hardy**
Tusenbach	**Derek Jacobi**		**Richard Kay**
Chebutikin	**Paul Curran**	Street musicians	**Helen Bourne**
Solloni	**Frank Wylie**		**Edward Roberts**

Production by	**Laurence Olivier**
Settings by	**Josef Svoboda**
Costumes by	**Beatrice Dawson**
Lighting by	**Richard Pilbrow**
Music & sound effects by	**Marc Wilkinson**
Special orchestrations by	**Derek Hudson**

Opening: 4 July 1967

THE ADVERTISEMENT

by Natalia Ginzburg, translated by Henry Reed

Teresa	**Joan Plowright**
Elena	**Anna Carteret**
Lorenzo	**Edward Petherbridge**
Giovanna	**Helen Bourne**
Production by	**Donald MacKechnie &**
	Laurence Olivier
Scenery & costumes by	**Patrick Robertson**
Lighting by	**Robert Ornbo**

Opening: 24 September 1968

HOME AND BEAUTY

by W Somerset Maugham

Miss Dennis	**Sheila Reid**
Victoria	**Geraldine McEwan**
Taylor	**Gabrielle Laye**
Mrs Shuttleworth	**Daphne Heard**
Mr Leicester Paton	**David Ryall**
Frederick Lowndes	**Robert Stephens**
William Cardew	**Robert Lang**
Nannie	**Margo Cunningham**
Mrs Pogson	**Mary Griffiths**
Mr A B Raham	**Laurence Olivier**
Miss Montmorency	**Jeanne Watts**
Clarence	**Christopher Reynalds**
Production by	**Frank Dunlop**
Scenery & costumes by	**Tom Lingwood**
Lighting by	**Robert Ornbo**

Opening: 8 October 1968; with LO: 30 January 1969

The National Theatre
works in association
with the Arts Council
of Great Britain

W Somerset Maugham

The National Theatre

at The
National Old Vic
Theatre

Seats from 3/- to 32/6
95 for sale on the day

"... vastly enjoyable
entertainment".

"... a splendid night
at the theatre".

LOVE'S LABOUR'S LOST

by William Shakespeare

Duke Ferdinand	**Derek Jacobi**	Boyet	**Philip Locke**
Longaville	**Roger Forbes**	Rosaline	**Joan Plowright**
Dumaine	**Richard Kay**	The Princess of France	**Louise Purnell**
Berowne	**Jeremy Brett**	Katherine	**Judy Wilson**
Moth	**Simon Cramond**	Maria	**Helen Bourne**
Sir Nathaniel	**Charles Kay**	A forester	**George Selway**
Holofernes	**Paul Curran**	Mercade	**Kenneth Mackintosh**
Costard	**John McEnery**		
Dull	**Gerald James**	Production by	**Laurence Olivier**
Don Adriano de Armado	**Ronald Pickup**	Scenery & costumes by	**Carl Toms**
Jaquenetta	**Sheila Reid**	Lighting by	**Richard Pilbrow**
First French lord	**Robert Tayman**	Music by	**Marc Wilkinson**
Second French lord	**Peter Winter**	Movement by	**Claude Chagrin**

Opening: 19 December 1968

THE MERCHANT OF VENICE

by William Shakespeare

The Duke of Venice	**Benjamin Whitrow**	Old Gobbo	**Harry Lomax**
The Prince of Morocco	**Tom Baker**	Servant to Antonio	**Lawrence Trimble**
The Prince of Arragon	**Charles Kay**	Leonardo	**Alan Dudley**
Antonio	**Anthony Nicholls**	Balthasar	**Michael Harding**
Bassanio	**Jeremy Brett**	Stephano	**Patrick Carter**
Solanio	**Michael Tudor Barnes**	Portia	**Joan Plowright**
Gratiano	**Derek Jacobi**	Nerissa	**Anna Carteret**
Salerio	**Richard Kay**	Servant to Portia	**Gillian Barge**
Lorenzo	**Malcolm Reid**	Jessica	**Jane Lapotaire**
Shylock	**Laurence Olivier**	Singers	**Laura Sarti**
Tubal	**Lewis Jones**		**Clare Walmesley**
Lancelot Gobbo	**Jim Dale**		

Officers, servants, etc: **Hugh Armstrong, Kate Coleridge, Michael Edgar, Sean Roantree, Lawrence Trimble, Paul Vousden**

Production by	**Jonathan Miller**
Designed by	**Julia Trevelyan Oman**
Lighting by	**Robert Ornbo**
Musical arrangements & original music by	**Carl Davis**

Opening: 28 April 1970

The National Theatre
at the New Theatre

By arrangement with Donald Albery   Box Office Telephone 836 3878   in repertoire
performance dates available from
the New Theatre Box Office
St Martin's Lane London WC2

Amphitryon 38
Jean Giraudoux

Constance Cummings   Christopher Plummer   Production
Richard Kay   Jeanne Watts   Laurence Olivier
Geraldine McEwan   Benjamin Whitrow   Scenery and Costumes
                                                    Malcolm Pride
                                                    Lighting
                                                    David Hersey

AMPHITRYON 38

by Jean Giraudoux, version from adaptations by
S N Behrman and Roger Gellert

Jupiter	**Christopher Plummer**
Mercury	**Richard Kay**
Trumpeter	**Benjamin Whitrow**
Warrior	**Philippe Monnet**
Sosios	**Richard Kay**
Amphitryon	**Christopher Plummer**
Alkmena	**Geraldine McEwan**
Eklissa	**Jeanne Watts**
Leda	**Constance Cummings**
Mime	**Philippe Monnet**
	Peter Smart

Production by	**Laurence Olivier**
Designed by	**Malcolm Pride**
Music by	**Marc Wilkinson**

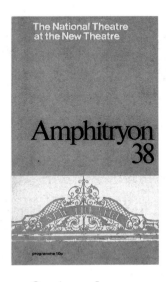

Opening: 23 June 1971

Long Day's Journey into Night

by Eugene O'Neill

James Tyrone	**Laurence Olivier**
Mary Cavan Tyrone	**Constance Cummings**
Jamie	**Denis Quilley**
Edmund	**Ronald Pickup**
Cathleen	**Jo Maxwell–Muller**
Production by	**Michael Blakemore**
Designed by	**Michael Annals**
Lighting by	**Robert Bryan**

The National Theatre

Opening: 21 December 1971

Long Day's Journey into Night

Eugene O'Neill

Constance Cummings
Rachel Davies
Laurence Olivier
Ronald Pickup
Denis Quilley

Production
Michael Blakemore

Scenery and Costumes
Michael Annals

Lighting
Robert Bryan

In repertoire
Performance details available from
The National Theatre Box Office
76 The Cut London SE1 8LP
01-928 7616

The National Theatre receives
financial assistance from the Arts
Council of Great Britain and the
Greater London Council

SATURDAY SUNDAY MONDAY

by Eduardo de Filippo,
English adaptation Keith Waterhouse and Willis Hall

Antonio	**Laurence Olivier**
Rosa	**Joan Plowright**
Peppino	**Frank Finlay**
Aunt Meme	**Mary Griffiths**
Attilio	**Martin Shaw**
Raffaele	**David Healy**
Roberto	**Gawn Grainger**
Rocco	**Nicholas Clay**
Guilianella	**Louise Purnell**
Federico	**Clive Merrison**
Maria	**Maggie Riley**
Luigi Ianniello	**Denis Quilley**
Elena	**Jeanne Watts**
Virginia	**Anna Carteret**
Michele	**Desmond McNamara**
Catiello	**Harry Lomax**
Dr Cefercola	**David Graham**
Directed by	**Franco Zeffirelli**
Settings by	**Franco Zeffirelli**
Costumes by	**Raimonda Gaetani**
Lighting by	**Leonard Tucker**
Musical arrangements by	**Michael Lankester**

Opening: 31 October 1973

THE PARTY

by Trevor Griffiths

Angie Shawcross	**Doran Godwin**
Joe Shawcross	**Ronald Pickup**
Eddie Shawcross	**John Shrapnel**
Milanka	**Sarah Atkinson**
Sloman	**Frank Finlay**
Andrew Ford	**Denis Quilley**
Kate Stead	**Rachel Davies**
Susie Plaistow	**Anna Carteret**
Louis Preece	**Ram John Holder**
Richard Maine	**Harry Waters**
'Grease' Ball	**Desmond McNamara**
Jeremy Hayes	**Gawn Grainger**
Kara Massingham	**Gillian Barge**
John Tagg	**Laurence Olivier**
Directed by	**John Dexter**
Designed by	**John Napier**
Lighting by	**Andy Phillips**
Projections by	**David Hersey**

Opening: 20 December 1973

EDEN END

by J B Priestley

Wilfred Kirby	**Paul Gregory**
Sarah	**Gabrielle Day**
Lilian Kirby	**Louie Ramsay**
Dr Kirby	**Leslie Sands**
Stella Kirby	**Joan Plowright**
Geoffrey Farrant	**Geoffrey Palmer**
Charles Appleby	**Michael Jayston**

and **Alan Brown, Kenneth de Carlo, Peter Jolley**

Directed by	**Laurence Olivier**
Designed by	**Carmen Dillon**
Lighting by	**Richard Pilbrow**
Additional music arrangements by	**Michael Lankester**

Opening: 4 April 1974

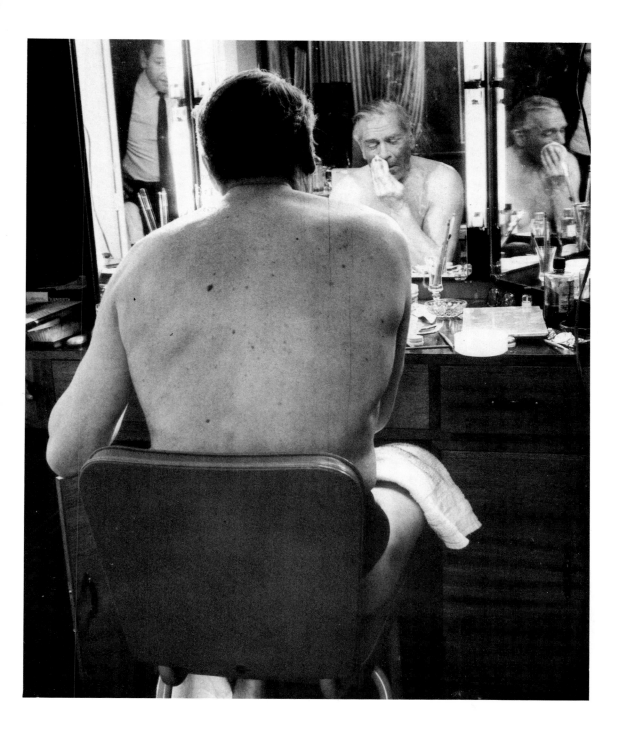

Olivier at Work first published in 1989 as a paperback original
jointly by the Royal National Theatre, London,
and Nick Hern Books, a division of Walker Books Limited,
87 Vauxhall Walk, London SE11 5HJ

Copyright ©1989 by the Royal National Theatre and
Nick Hern Books

First published in 1990 in the
United States of America by
Routledge/Theatre Arts Books
an imprint of Routledge, Chapman and Hall, Inc.
29 West 35 Street, New York, NY 10001

Cover Photo by Zoë Dominic

Library of Congress
Cataloguing – in Publication Data
Olivier at Work
A Theatre Arts book
First published in 1990
jointly by Theatre Arts/Routledge
and Nick Hern Books

1. Olivier, Laurence, 1907-1989 -- Criticism and
interpretation. 2. Royal National Theatre (London,
England) -- History. I. Olivier, Richard. II. Plowright,
Joan. III. Haill, Lyn. IV. Royal National Theatre
(London, England).
PN2598.O55O38 1990   792'028'092   89-70105

ISBN 0-87830-096-1

Designed by David Fordham and Carol McCleeve

Printed and bound in Great Britain by Jolly and Barber Ltd,
Rugby